The Origin of Puccini the Cat

Copyright © 2024 Charlotte Lily Gaspard

Coolgrove Press, an imprint of
Cool Grove Publishing, Inc. New York.
512 Argyle Road, Brooklyn, NY 11218
All rights reserved under the International and
Pan-American Copyright Conventions.

www.coolgrove.com
For permissions and other inquiries write to info@coolgrove.com

ISBN 13: 978-1-887276-47-4
Library of Congress Control Number: 2020945385

This book is dedicated to all the Spirit Animals
especially Puccini and Theodore Luck Dragon
and the children of planet Earth

Media alchemy by Kiku

Coolgrove Press

The Origin of Puccini the Cat

by Charlotte Lily Gaspard

Once upon a time,
in a land far, far away,
on a planet far, far away,
there was an extraordinary Dream Cat named:

Giacomo
Antonio
Domenico
Michelle
Secundo
Maria
Puccini.

On the planet where Puccini lived, the main interest was the study of dreams, and he was one of the most well-respected researchers in this field.

He was the President of the Dreamers Institute, a place completely dedicated to the science of dreams and their meanings.

Puccini was a best-selling author on the subject. He gave many lectures that were always filled with the best minds in the galaxy.

Puccini was also a favorite of the Royal Family. They would often host parties and wonderful feasts in his honor.

Puccini had everything

except that which his heart desired the most...

The love of the Princess.

Puccini and the Princess had many excuses to spend time together. She was a great philosopher who read many books.

They would take long walks together away from the castle until they reached the forest, where they could be alone except for the birds and the trees.

One day, when they were taking one of their walks, Puccini could not bear it anymore. He decided to tell his beloved Princess the truth.

"Princess, I have been meaning to speak with you for some time. I may seem to have everything I could desire, but the only thing I truly want is to spend my life with you."

"Oh, Giacomo!" the Princess exclaimed.
Although she was surprised, she was glad.
She would like nothing better than to marry Puccini and be with him always.
They both knew this could not be,
for it was forbidden.

Puccini was not of the Royal Family,
and the Princess was already betrothed
to another of the King's choosing.

So they decided
to keep their love
a secret.

Some time later, Puccini was walking alone through the forest. As we all know, cats like to catch birds. Usually on his walks he was with the Princess, so he would not even notice the temptation of the innocent birds fluttering about in the trees.

On this day, Puccini was feeling restless, and a little sad. He could not have the company of the Princess, for she would be busy inside the castle for the whole afternoon.

A beautiful Blue Bird flew by...

Puccini pounced on it, and caught the bird fast between his paws. The Blue Bird squawked and struggled but it could not get free.

"Please," the bird squeaked.
"Please don't hurt me with those sharp claws!"

"I am a cat. I must do what cats do. I have caught you and now I will break your wings so you cannot fly away."

"No, please!" the Blue Bird sang. "You may be a cat, but I know you are a romantic. I have seen you walking with your true love and I know your heart beats for beauty and freedom.
If you break my wings, I shall never fly again, and flying is the most wonderful feeling of beauty and freedom there is.
I know you care about these things, for you could not love the Princess the way that you do if you had no compassion!"

Puccini still held the bird, but he was careful not to prick its feathers with his sharp claws.

They were silent a long moment, while each listened to their own breath, their own heart beating.

Finally, Puccini spoke.

"Little Blue Bird, I have never spoken to a bird about love before.
It is true - as my heart is filled with thoughts of the Princess all other
things have become more beautiful to me. And freedom was something
I never considered before now. If I were free to follow my destiny
I would be with the Princess always."

Puccini opened up his paws and let the Blue Bird fly free.
It spread its perfect tiny wings and made off for the blue of the sky.

Puccini sighed, sad to see the Bird disappear so quickly.

He continued on through the forest until he came to a hollow by
a tree. Naptime overtook him, so he lay down to rest.

He is a cat, after all,
and a Dream Cat, at that.

Soon he was asleep.

Suddenly the clearing was filled with such a fluttering and flapping! Puccini awakened, surrounded by more birds than he had ever seen before. They were every different color and shape and size. Among them was his new friend, the Blue Bird.
The fluttering and flapping finally calmed, and a very grand Pink Flamingo approached Puccini on his rock.

"Ahem, sir. We desire an audience with you. Never before has a cat let a bird go free. We are very impressed with you. My associate here tells me you are trapped in a secret love affair and cannot be with your sweetheart. We would like to help you."

And so Puccini stayed with the Birds for some time, plotting and scheming ways to overcome the obstacles blocking him from a life with the Princess.

And life went on, much as it had before. Except now the Princess
and Puccini had hope. For the birds can fly!
And the birds believe deeply in beauty and freedom.

The two continued to sneak away to the forest where they could be
alone together. They believed that no one noticed them.
But cats are very observant creatures, and Puccini was not the only
one who loved the Princess. Soon the cats in the Royal Court began to
notice the growing friendship between Puccini and the Princess,
and they began to talk.
This caused more talk, for that is the way of gossip.
As one jealous cat spoke to another, and another, and another,
the story of their love twisted and became ugly.

Before long,
someone decided to tell the King.

The King was furious and called Puccini before him.

"Puccini! I thought you to be my most loyal subject, and now I hear you are carrying on an affair with my daughter! Right underneath my whiskers!"

There was nothing Puccini could say. He would not deny his love for the Princess, or his desire to marry her.

The King was so angry he locked Puccini in a cage.

The King stormed off to find the Princess
so he could confront her.

"Daughter! You have been betrothed since
before you were born!
Would you dare defy my wishes?"

Again there was nothing the Princess could say.
She would not lie to her father, the King.

For punishment he sent the Princess away to a tower
overlooking the sea.

It is a mean thing to lock a princess in a tower away from the world. It is an especially mean thing to do to a cat princess, for the only view she had was the sky and the waves.

Cats cannot fly, and they are afraid of the water.

The King stormed about for some time
and had a few birds kidnapped.

Then he felt just a little bit better.
He had an idea of what he would do to Puccini.

The King commanded a ship to be built like none ever seen before on the planet of the Dream Cats.

He called his best cat scientists to the task. They went to work; with knowledge gained from the unfortunate birds who were prisoners.

Time passed.

Puccini sat brooding in his cage,
longing for the Princess.

The Princess paced in her tower
overlooking the sea,
missing Puccini terribly.

Soon enough, Puccini found himself before the King one more time.

"Puccini! For your betrayal, there is only one punishment that will fit the crime. You shall be banished, never to return to us."

Puccini was led to the ship, his heart heavy.

Far away in the distance, the Princess watched from her tower and saw a great blast of smoke and a grand blaze of light as the ship carrying Puccini flew up! up! up! into the sky and away from her.

"What shall I do?
How shall I ever find him again?"

Let us never forget that Dream Cats are mystical creatures with magical powers. Although Puccini and the Princess are far apart from each other now, they can always visit in their dreams...
So they will never truly be separated.

Hopefully, they shall find their way back to each other.
They will both certainly try, which is a very good start.
But that is a tale for another day.

TO BE CONTINUED....

All of the images in this book are based on handmade Shadow Puppets.

They are featured in performances and more by our theatre collective Midnight Radio Show.

In the following pages, you can

Learn How To Make Your Own Shadow Puppet!

Materials & Supplies:
paper
scissors
pen or pencil or marker
a stick
tape
a flashlight
hole puncher (optional)

Draw your shape.

Cut out the shape
Or ask a grownup to cut it for you.

Tape your shape to a stick.

If you have a hole puncher, you can decorate your shape with dots.

Shine the flashlight on your shape, and...

Now you have a Shadow Puppet!

"Part celestial creature, part sophisticated human" is how Charlotte Lily Gaspard has been described by Enchanted Living Magazine when contemplating the ethereal artist and her work in one of their features. Shadow puppet artist, educator, entertainer, and "bona fide fairy princess" (DUMBO Living), Charlotte's mission is to activate imaginations and celebrate playfulness wherever she goes.

Charlotte is the founder and artistic director of Midnight Radio Show, a shadow puppet sci-fi fairytale theatre collective based in Brooklyn, NYC. Charlotte and her collective are known for devising innovative avant-garde enchantments, infused with puppets, poetry, music and dance, for the stage and beyond.

They have received funding and support from the Jim Henson Foundation, Brooklyn Arts Council, A.R.T./New York, the New York Restoration Project, along with commissions and residencies at La MaMa Experimental Theater Club, Make Art With Purpose, and Handmade Puppet Dreams, among others.

Theatre Collective: www.MidnightRadioShow.org
Watch videos: www.MidnightRadioShow.tv
Projects: www.CharlotteGaspard.com